Waiting for Baby

A Pregnancy Memory Album

TRACEY CLARK

CHRONICLE BOOKS
SAN FRANCISCO

ISBN 978-0-8118-3672-2
Designed by Lisa Billard Design, NYC

Manufactured in China

20 19 18 17 16 15 14 13 12 11

Chronicle Books LLC
680 Second Street
San Francisco, CA 94107
www.chroniclebooks.com

Select vintage wallpapers courtesy of Second Hand Rose, NYC

acknowledgments

From the beginning, I have been surrounded by an incredible network of family and friends, each of whom uniquely contributed to the fruition of this project. To every one of them, I would like to express my appreciation and deepest affections. And a special thank you to Carey Jones and Deidre Knight; both to whom I am forever grateful.

To my husband, Alexis, whose never ending love and support delight and inspire me every minute of every day.

And lastly, to Julia, my beautiful daughter and brightest star. I dedicate this book to her.

an introduction

Carrying a growing baby within one's own body marks the beginning of something both magical and miraculous, something so moving and so complex that I find it impossible to compare it to anything I have ever known. Pregnancy is not simply a means to an end, but is one of the most intimate journeys a woman can take. This book was designed to honor that journey.

During my own pregnancy, I was exhilarated and frightened in the same breath. Surprised to find myself overtaken by this flood of conflicting emotions, I wrote fervently in my journal for nine months straight. Through this form of expression, I found great comfort and inner guidance. With every word, I was telling my story, creating my own history. What I wrote then, I treasure now as a priceless chronology of my personal passage into motherhood.

My experience drove me to develop this book. My hope is that it inspires you to record your own pregnancy story. By writing and reflecting on this incredible time in your life, you will grow and evolve as a person, a woman, and a soon-to-be mommy.

Experience, appreciate, and live this journey. It is one of the most amazing trips you'll ever take.

And then, motherhood begins.

table of contents

mother-to-be

"When you begin, begin at the beginning, begin with magic, begin with the sun, begin with grass."

—Helen Wolfert

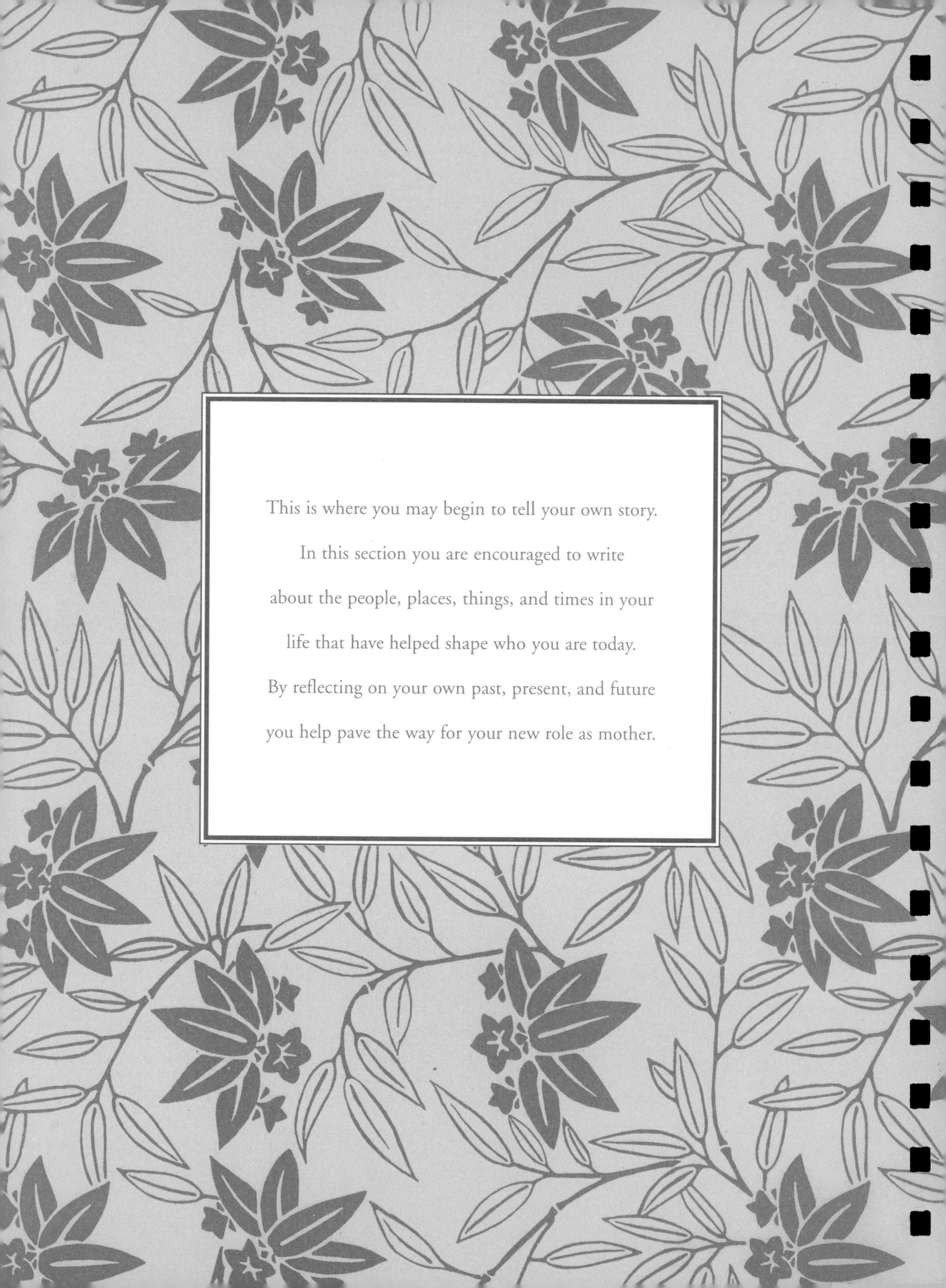

This is where you may begin to tell your own story.

In this section you are encouraged to write

about the people, places, things, and times in your

life that have helped shape who you are today.

By reflecting on your own past, present, and future

you help pave the way for your new role as mother.

my story

How I first found out I was pregnant

Some of my initial thoughts and feelings about expecting a new baby

Details on how and when I first shared the news with family and friends

Their reactions, thoughts, and feelings

my history

When and where I was born

space for my baby photograph

When and where this photograph was taken

Stories I have been told of my own birth

Some of my life's highlights

my family tree

me/birthdate

my mother/birthdate

my father/birthdate

maternal grandmother/
birthdate

maternal grandfather/
birthdate

paternal grandmother/
birthdate

paternal grandfather/
birthdate

maternal great grandmother/birthdate

maternal great grandfather/birthdate

paternal great grandmother/birthdate

paternal great grandfather/birthdate

maternal great grandmother/birthdate

maternal great grandfather/birthdate

paternal great grandmother/birthdate

paternal great grandfather/birthdate

me

space for recent photograph of myself

When and where this photograph was taken

Where I'm living

My line of work

Things I enjoy

Things I value

Places I go

My favorites (music, books, television, movies . . .)

My strengths and weaknesses

Some of my life's goals

good friends and family

People who are important to me

space for photographs of my family and friends

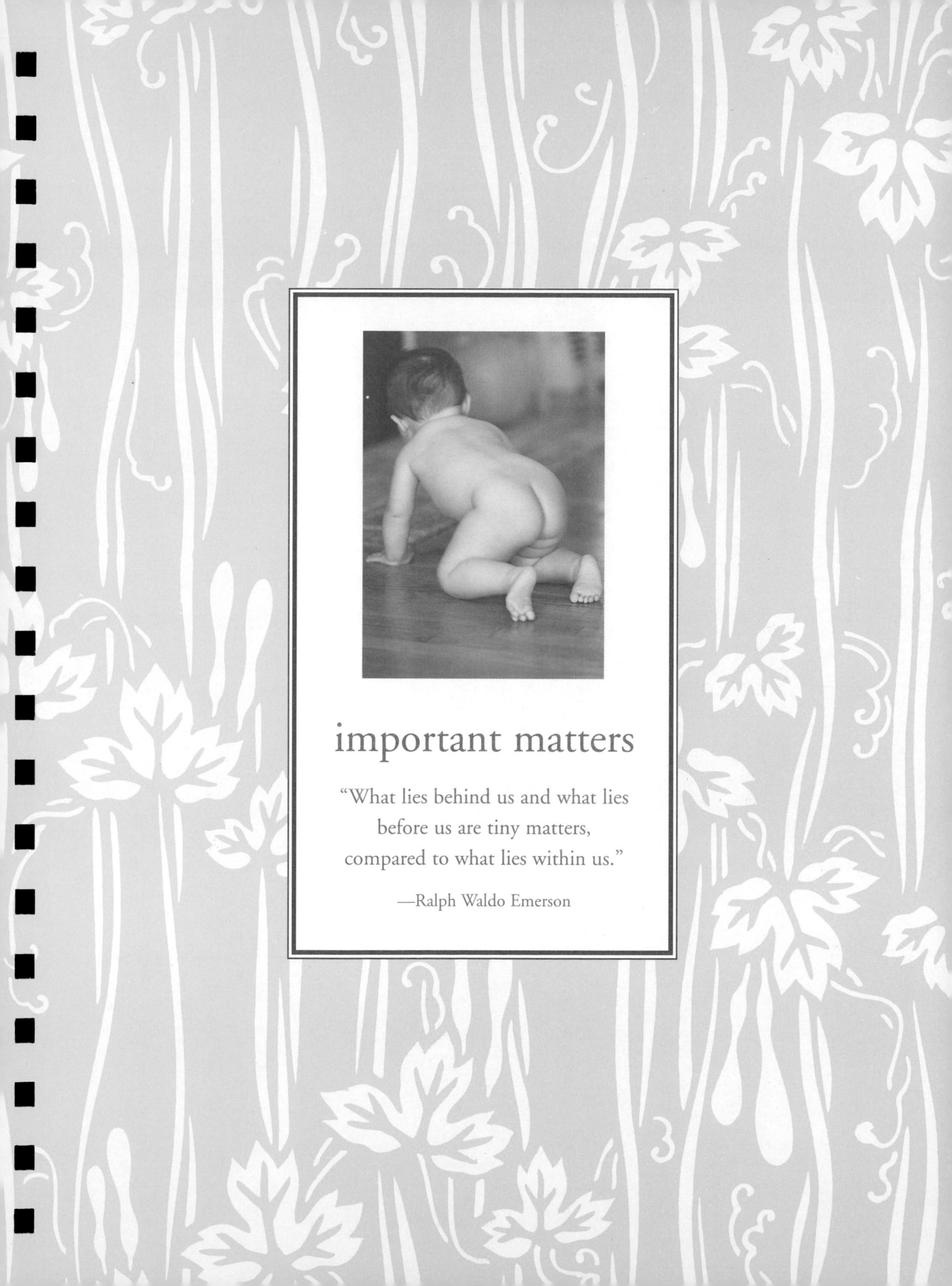
important matters
"What lies behind us and what lies
before us are tiny matters,
compared to what lies within us."
—Ralph Waldo Emerson

Besides the birth of a precious new baby, the next nine months will provide you with a number of highlights. Use this section to record the unique events of your own pregnancy experience, and ensure that these memorable moments will never be forgotten.

my pregnancy

My hopes and dreams for my pregnancy

What I'm looking forward to

Things I am hesitant about

What excites me the most about being pregnant

significant others

People who will play an important role throughout my pregnancy and why

Thoughts and feelings about these special people and the roles they will play

doctor/midwife visit

Week

Procedures performed

My progress (health, weight, or anything noteworthy . . .)

Baby's progress (growth, movement, or anything noteworthy . . .)

Thoughts and feelings about the visit

Things to remember

doctor/midwife visit

Week

Procedures performed

My progress

Baby's progress

Thoughts and feelings about the visit

Things to remember

doctor/midwife visit

Week

Procedures performed

My progress

Baby's progress

Thoughts and feelings about the visit

Things to remember

doctor/midwife visit

Week

Procedures performed

My progress

Baby's progress

Thoughts and feelings about the visit

Things to remember

doctor/midwife visit

Week

Procedures performed

My progress

Baby's progress

Thoughts and feelings about the visit

Things to remember

doctor/midwife visit

Week

Procedures performed

My progress

Baby's progress

Thoughts and feelings about the visit

Things to remember

doctor/midwife visit

Week

Procedures performed

My progress

Baby's progress

Thoughts and feelings about the visit

Things to remember

doctor/midwife visit

Week

Procedures performed

My progress

Baby's progress

Thoughts and feelings about the visit

Things to remember

doctor/midwife visit

Week

Procedures performed

My progress

Baby's progress

Thoughts and feelings about the visit

Things to remember

doctor/midwife visit

Week

Procedures performed

My progress

Baby's progress

Thoughts and feelings about the visit

Things to remember

doctor/midwife visit

Week

Procedures performed

My progress

Baby's progress

Thoughts and feelings about the visit

Things to remember

doctor/midwife visit

Week

Procedures performed

My progress

Baby's progress

Thoughts and feelings about the visit

Things to remember

doctor/midwife visit

Week

Procedures performed

My progress

Baby's progress

Thoughts and feelings about the visit

Things to remember

doctor/midwife visit

Week

Procedures performed

My progress

Baby's progress

Thoughts and feelings about the visit

Things to remember

doctor/midwife visit

Week

Procedures performed

My progress

Baby's progress

Thoughts and feelings about the visit

Things to remember

doctor/midwife visit

Week

Procedures performed

My progress

Baby's progress

Thoughts and feelings about the visit

Things to remember

first impressions *prenatal images*

Date/Week

space for ultrasound image

What the image shows/Technician's comments

My reaction to seeing the baby

Baby's activity during ultrasound

Reactions of others who were there

Highlights of the visit

My thoughts and feelings about the experience

space for additional images from the visit

first impressions *prenatal images*

Date/Week

space for ultrasound image

What the image shows/Technician's comments

My reaction to seeing the baby

Baby's activity during ultrasound

Reactions of others who were there

Highlights of the visit

My thoughts and feelings about the experience

space for additional images from the visit

pregnancy firsts *dates and details of my pregnancy milestones*

First minute I thought I was pregnant and my first thoughts

First person I told and when

First book I bought and read

First doctor/midwife visit and how I felt

First time I heard the baby's heartbeat and how I felt

First time I really felt pregnant

First craving I had

First aversion I had

First day I felt tired/sick and what my symptoms were

First time I noticed my belly

First time someone else noticed my belly

First time I wore "maternity" clothes and what they were

First time I felt the baby and what the sensation was like

First time I felt a real kick and my reaction

Fist time someone else felt a kick and their reaction

First time I saw the baby kick and my reaction

First time I felt Braxton-Hicks and how it felt

First outfit I bought for baby

First toy I bought for baby

First piece of furniture I bought for baby

First gift I got from someone

First time I felt like "it might be time" to have the baby

Baby's birthday

body and mind

"Everything's changing
while the day sky stays blue."

—Karen Peris

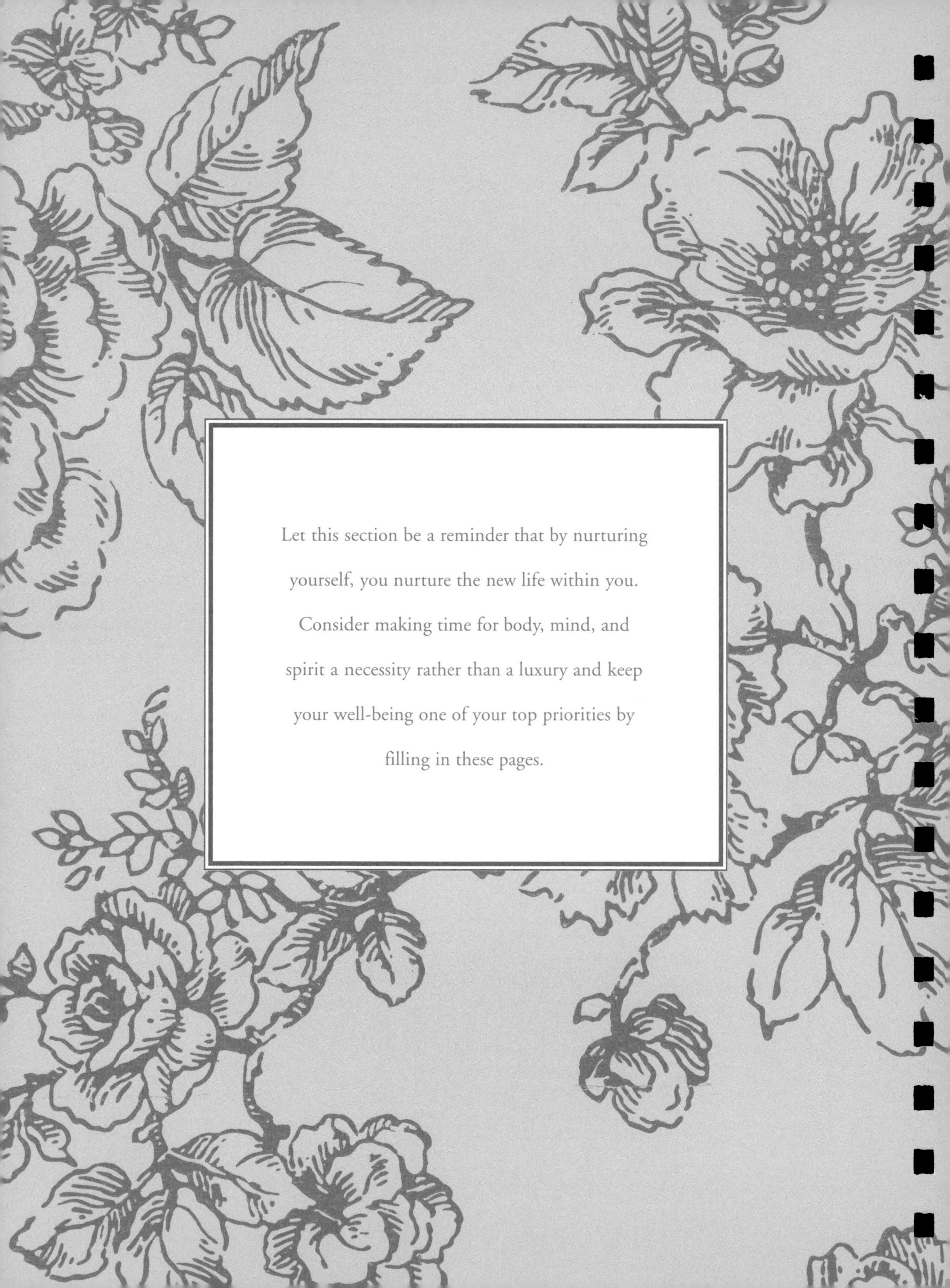

Let this section be a reminder that by nurturing yourself, you nurture the new life within you. Consider making time for body, mind, and spirit a necessity rather than a luxury and keep your well-being one of your top priorities by filling in these pages.

my pregnancy photographs

There has never been a more appropriate time to show off your beautiful body. Have friends or family help you document your progress by taking photographs of you throughout your pregnancy journey. You'll enjoy the whole progression, so start even before you're "showing". Consider hiring a professional photographer closer to the end of your pregnancy to artistically capture your glow. Don't forget to date each photograph.

space for photographs of me throughout my pregnancy

space for more photographs

space for more photographs

taking care of me *my first trimester*

Things I'm doing now to nurture myself

Things I'm taking pleasure in

What I do in my alone time

Finding time to rest

What I'm reading/Things I'm learning

Things I'm doing to keep myself strong and healthy

Things I'm doing to prepare my body and mind for labor and delivery

Reflections

taking care of me *my second trimester*

Things I'm doing now to nurture myself

Things I'm taking pleasure in

What I do in my alone time

Finding time to rest

What I'm reading/Things I'm learning

Things I'm doing to keep myself strong and healthy

Things I'm doing to prepare my body and mind for labor and delivery

Reflections

taking care of me *my third trimester*

Things I'm doing now to nurture myself

Things I'm taking pleasure in

What I do in my alone time

Finding time to rest

What I'm reading/Things I'm learning

Things I'm doing to keep myself strong and healthy

Things I'm doing to prepare my body and mind for labor and delivery

Reflections

my body *progress page*

Date/Week

Belly measurement/Weight

My physical progress

How I'm feeling about my body

Cravings and aversions

Energy level

Baby movement

my mind

Thoughts, feelings, emotions

Excitements and anxieties

Things that make me laugh

Things that make me cry

Things I'm learning about myself

my body *progress page*

Date/Week

Belly measurement/Weight

My physical progress

How I'm feeling about my body

Cravings and aversions

Energy level

Baby movement

my mind

Thoughts, feelings, emotions

Excitements and anxieties

Things that make me laugh

Things that make me cry

Things I'm learning about myself

my body *progress page*

Date/Week

Belly measurement/Weight

My physical progress

How I'm feeling about my body

Cravings and aversions

Energy level

Baby movement

my mind

Thoughts, feelings, emotions

Excitements and anxieties

Things that make me laugh

Things that make me cry

Things I'm learning about myself

my body *progress page*

Date/Week

Belly measurement/Weight

My physical progress

How I'm feeling about my body

Cravings and aversions

Energy level

Baby movement

my mind

Thoughts, feelings, emotions

Excitements and anxieties

Things that make me laugh

Things that make me cry

Things I'm learning about myself

my body *progress page*

Date/Week

Belly measurement/Weight

My physical progress

How I'm feeling about my body

Cravings and aversions

Energy level

Baby movement

my mind

Thoughts, feelings, emotions

Excitements and anxieties

Things that make me laugh

Things that make me cry

Things I'm learning about myself

my body *progress page*

Date/Week

Belly measurement/Weight

My physical progress

How I'm feeling about my body

Cravings and aversions

Energy level

Baby movement

my mind

Thoughts, feelings, emotions

Excitements and anxieties

Things that make me laugh

Things that make me cry

Things I'm learning about myself

my body *progress page*

Date/Week

Belly measurement/Weight

My physical progress

How I'm feeling about my body

Cravings and aversions

Energy level

Baby movement

my mind

Thoughts, feelings, emotions

Excitements and anxieties

Things that make me laugh

Things that make me cry

Things I'm learning about myself

my body *progress page*

Date/Week

Belly measurement/Weight

My physical progress

How I'm feeling about my body

Cravings and aversions

Energy level

Baby movement

my mind

Thoughts, feelings, emotions

Excitements and anxieties

Things that make me laugh

Things that make me cry

Things I'm learning about myself

my body *progress page*

Date/Week

Belly measurement/Weight

My physical progress

How I'm feeling about my body

Cravings and aversions

Energy level

Baby movement

my mind

Thoughts, feelings, emotions

Excitements and anxieties

Things that make me laugh

Things that make me cry

Things I'm learning about myself

Additional notes:

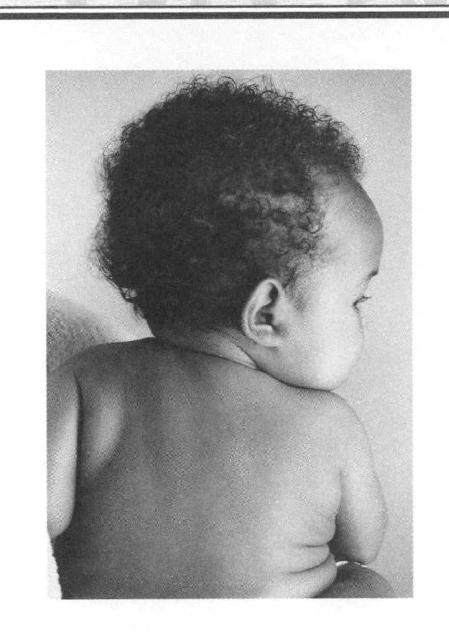

preparations

"Life is always a rich and steady time
when you are waiting for
something to happen or hatch."

—E.B. White

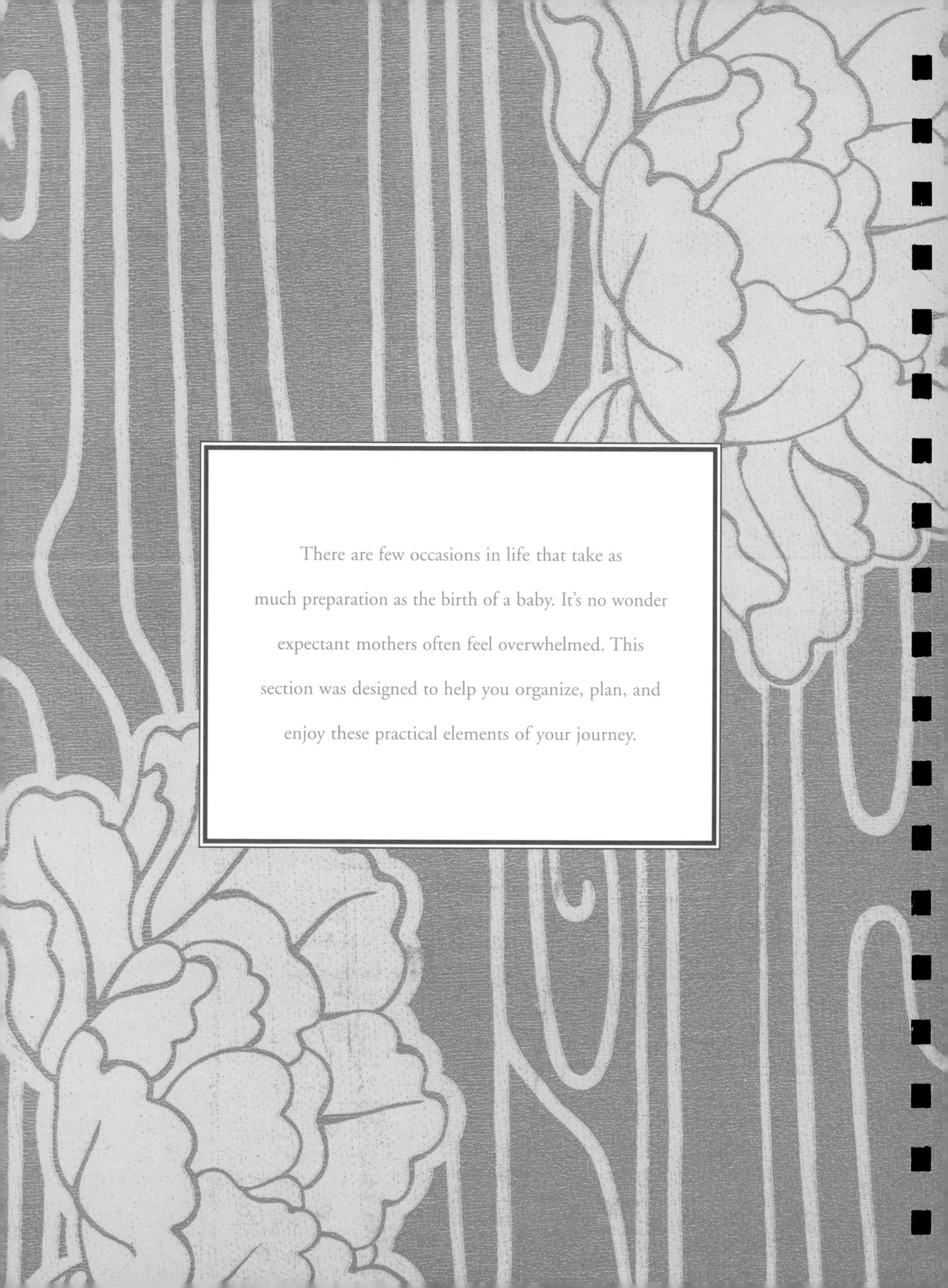

There are few occasions in life that take as much preparation as the birth of a baby. It's no wonder expectant mothers often feel overwhelmed. This section was designed to help you organize, plan, and enjoy these practical elements of your journey.

baby names

Nicknames for unborn baby

First names to consider

Middle names to consider

Final name chosen for girl

Comments or thoughts on why this name was chosen

Final name chosen for boy

Comments or thoughts on why this name was chosen

nursery notes

My hopes and dreams for the baby's nursery

Ideas and thoughts on color choices/theme/vibe of nursery

Furniture I have

Furniture I need

Other details

nursery wishes

clippings, swatches, pictures, or notes for baby's space

baby's space *the nursery's progression*

Date photograph was taken

space for photograph of baby's space

Notes:

Date photograph was taken

space for photograph of baby's space

Notes:

learning

Class I'm taking

Thoughts on what I'm learning

Points to remember

References

Friends made/Contact information

Class I'm taking

Thoughts on what I'm learning

Points to remember

References

Friends made/Contact information

birth plan

My coach/support/advocate during labor

My hopes for my labor and delivery experience

My priorities during labor and delivery

The atmosphere I'd like to create for my labor and delivery

Tools I plan to use during labor and delivery (visualizations, focal points, mantras, affirmations, music)

Notes:

Additional notes:

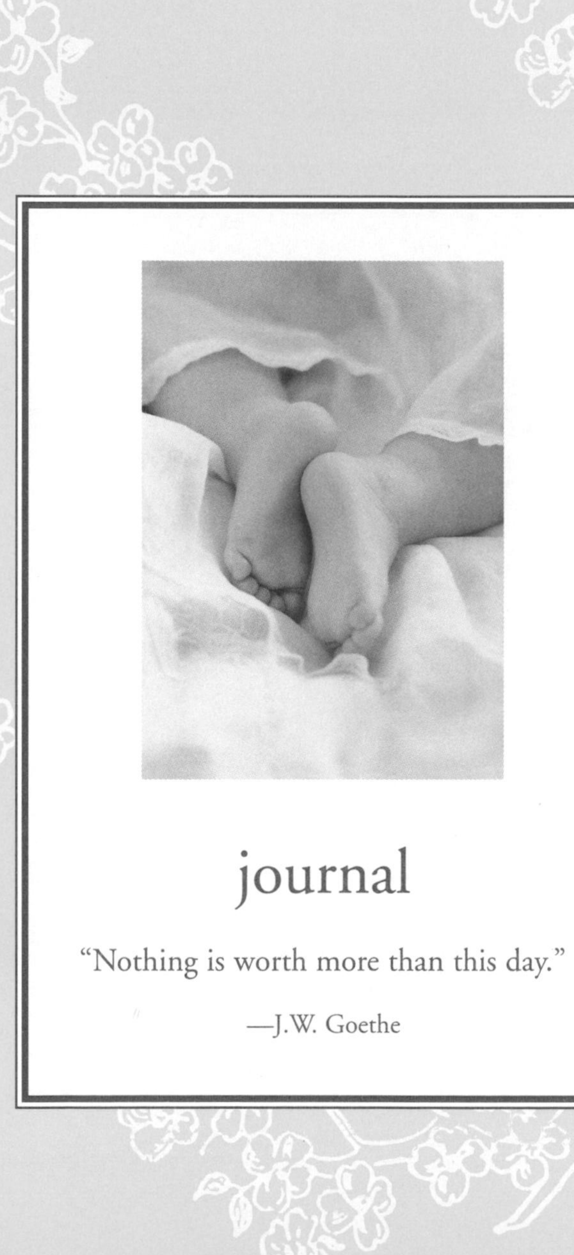
journal
"Nothing is worth more than this day."
—J.W. Goethe

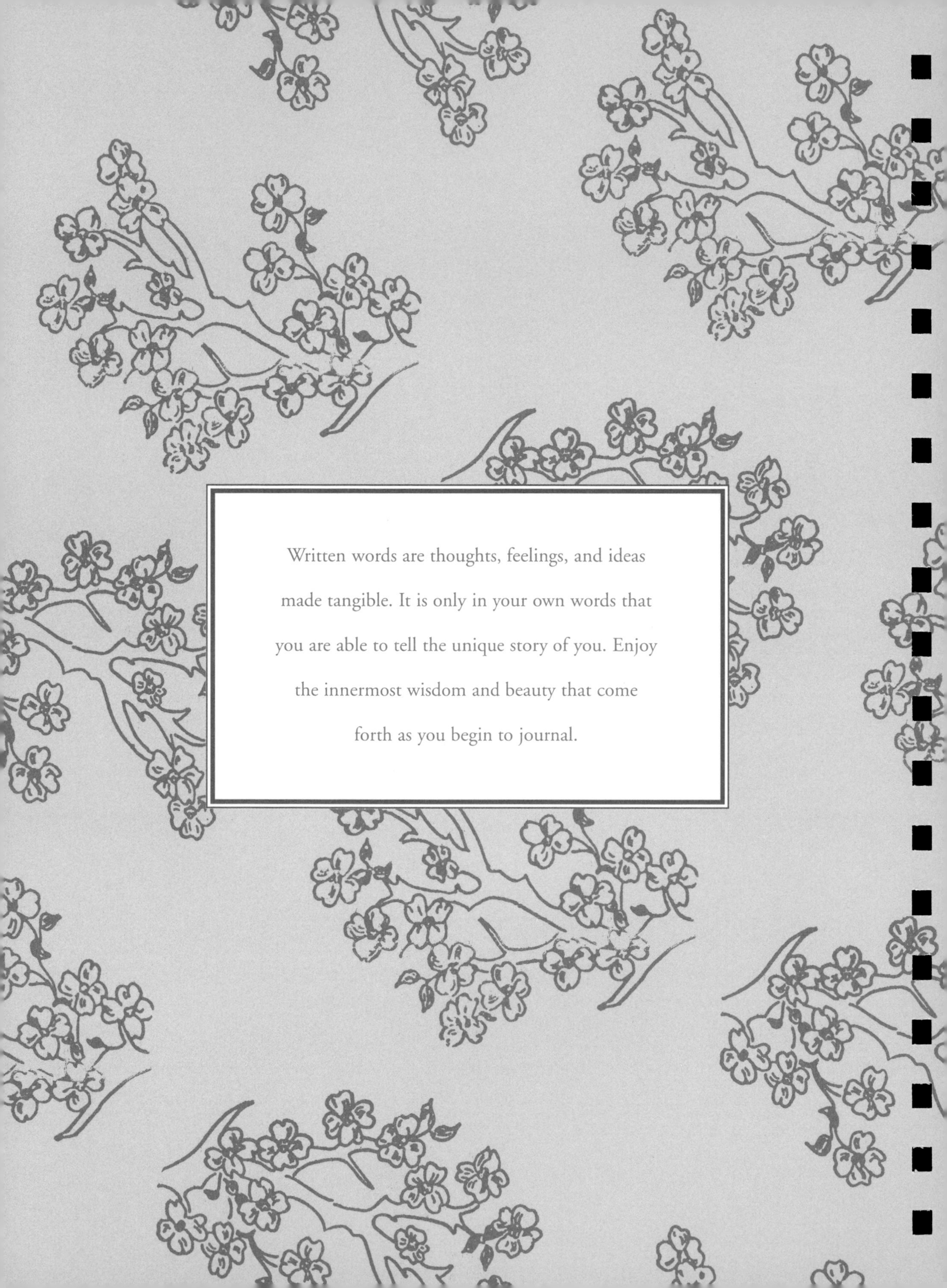

Written words are thoughts, feelings, and ideas made tangible. It is only in your own words that you are able to tell the unique story of you. Enjoy the innermost wisdom and beauty that come forth as you begin to journal.

dreaming of baby *my dreams throughout pregnancy*

Date/Dream

Reflections

Date/Dream

Reflections

Date/Dream

Reflections

Date/Dream

Reflections

Date/Dream

Reflections

Date/Dream

Reflections

my journal

From your daily comings and goings to your most personal thoughts, the lined pages that follow give you the space to write it all down.

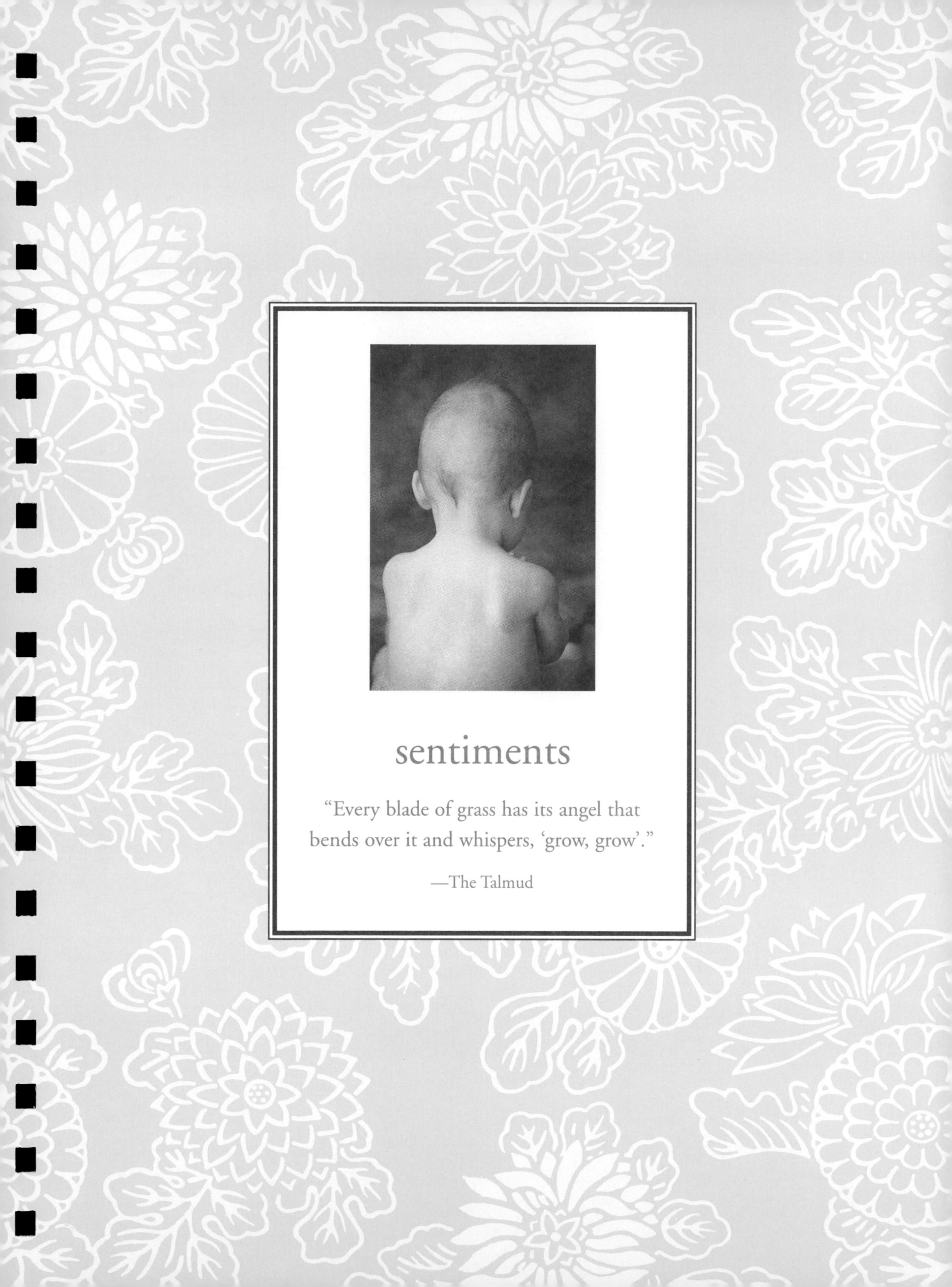

sentiments

"Every blade of grass has its angel that bends over it and whispers, 'grow, grow'."

—The Talmud

News of a coming baby can bring with it a multitude of well wishes. By these sentiments, you are reminded of how much you and your baby are loved. This is a place for these special gestures.

well wishes

space for cards, notes, or letters received

space for cards, notes, or letters received

space for cards, notes, or letters received

special deliveries *gifts received by mail*

Gift given/Sent by

Thoughts and feelings

Gift given/Sent by

Thoughts and feelings

Gift given/Sent by

Thoughts and feelings

Gift given/Sent by

Thoughts and feelings

Gift given/Sent by

Thoughts and feelings

baby blessings *wishes, hopes, and dreams dedicated to baby*

These can be sentiments for baby from you or from family and friends, in any form. Perhaps you have a favorite poem or quote that you wish to record here. You could ask someone special to compose a letter especially for baby or simply share a story or kind comment someone made.

dear baby *a letter to my child*

Date

dear baby *a letter to my child*

Date

celebrations

"Waiting for you to arrive,
where does the time go?"

—Karen Peris

There will come a time in your pregnancy when friends and family will gather to celebrate and honor you as you approach your new or renewed role as mother. These gestures of affection are also sending the message to baby: "We love and welcome you to the world." Use this space to remember the celebrations.

celebrating *baby showers and other celebrations*

Date/Location

Hostess

space for invitation

Guests

Menu

Special activities

Special gifts given

Reflections on the celebration

celebrating *baby showers and other celebrations*

Date/Location

Hostess

space for invitation

Guests

Menu

Special activities

Special gifts given

Reflections on the celebration

celebrating *baby showers and other celebrations*

Date/Location

Hostess

space for invitation

Guests

Menu

Special activities

Special gifts given

Reflections on the celebration

space for cards or photographs

space for cards or photographs

space for cards or photographs

space for cards or photographs

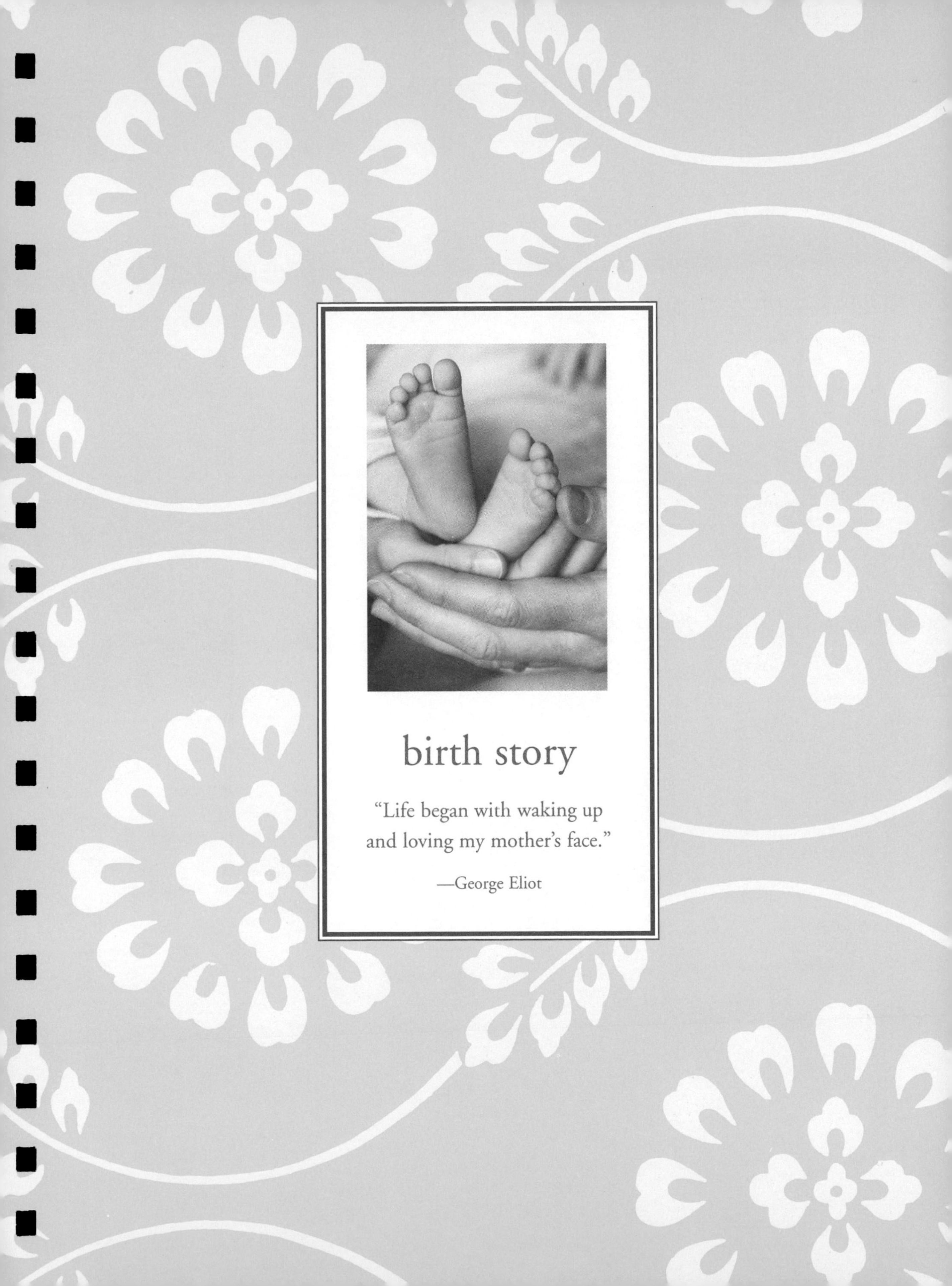
birth story
"Life began with waking up
and loving my mother's face."
—George Eliot

Although the journey of pregnancy ends here, the journey of motherhood is just beginning. The last nine months have been preparing you for the moment of giving birth to your new baby. This is a moment you'll want to remember forever. On these pages you are encouraged to write down every detail.

labor

First signs of labor

Date/Time

Thoughts and feelings

Details about the beginning stages of labor

All those who accompanied and assisted me throughout labor

What they did to help/encourage/support

Tools I used during labor (focal points, visualization, atmosphere, etc.)

My strengths and weaknesses while laboring

turning points

Details on my labor stages/transitions/turning points

Memorable moments

Details about the delivery

My feelings and first reaction to baby's birth

The first minutes with baby

the baby *a new little life*

Name

Gender/Height and weight

Time and date of birth

Notes on baby's overall health/APGAR score

First impressions

space for baby's first photograph

Hair, eyes, and nose

Fingers and toes

Birthmarks

Resemblances

Cry

Disposition

first things first

These spaces are for you to write about some of baby's "firsts", how baby reacted, and how the experience felt to you.

First feeding

Baby's very first bath

First diaper change

First calls made to share the news

introducing baby

Family and friends who were there to greet baby

Their reactions to meeting baby

Memorable moments

our stay at the hospital

Visitors and phone calls

Meals

Sleeping arrangements

Where and how baby slept

Help from the staff

Memorable moments

space for cards or photographs

space for cards or photographs

my physical well-being

How my body feels since the delivery

Doctor/Midwife advice

Nursing notes

my emotional well-being

How it feels not to be pregnant

How it feels to be a mother

My emotions

My overall state-of-mind

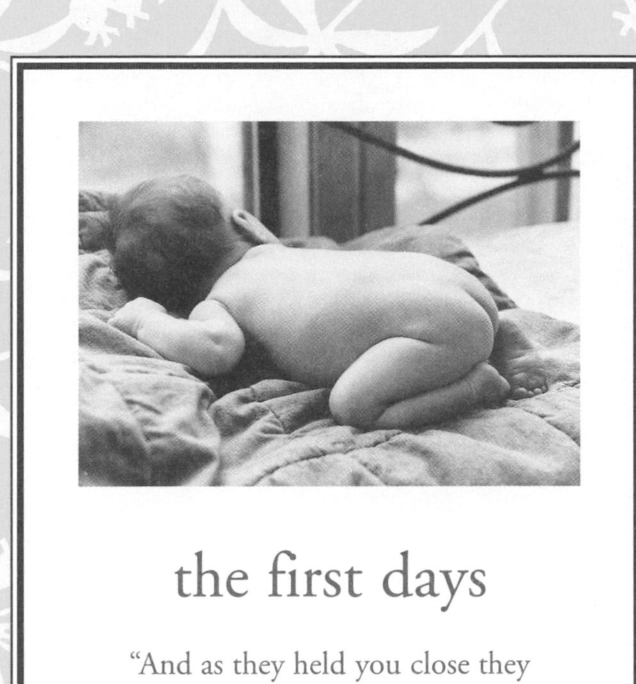

the first days

"And as they held you close they
whispered into your open curving ear,
'We are so glad you've come!'"

—Debra Frasier

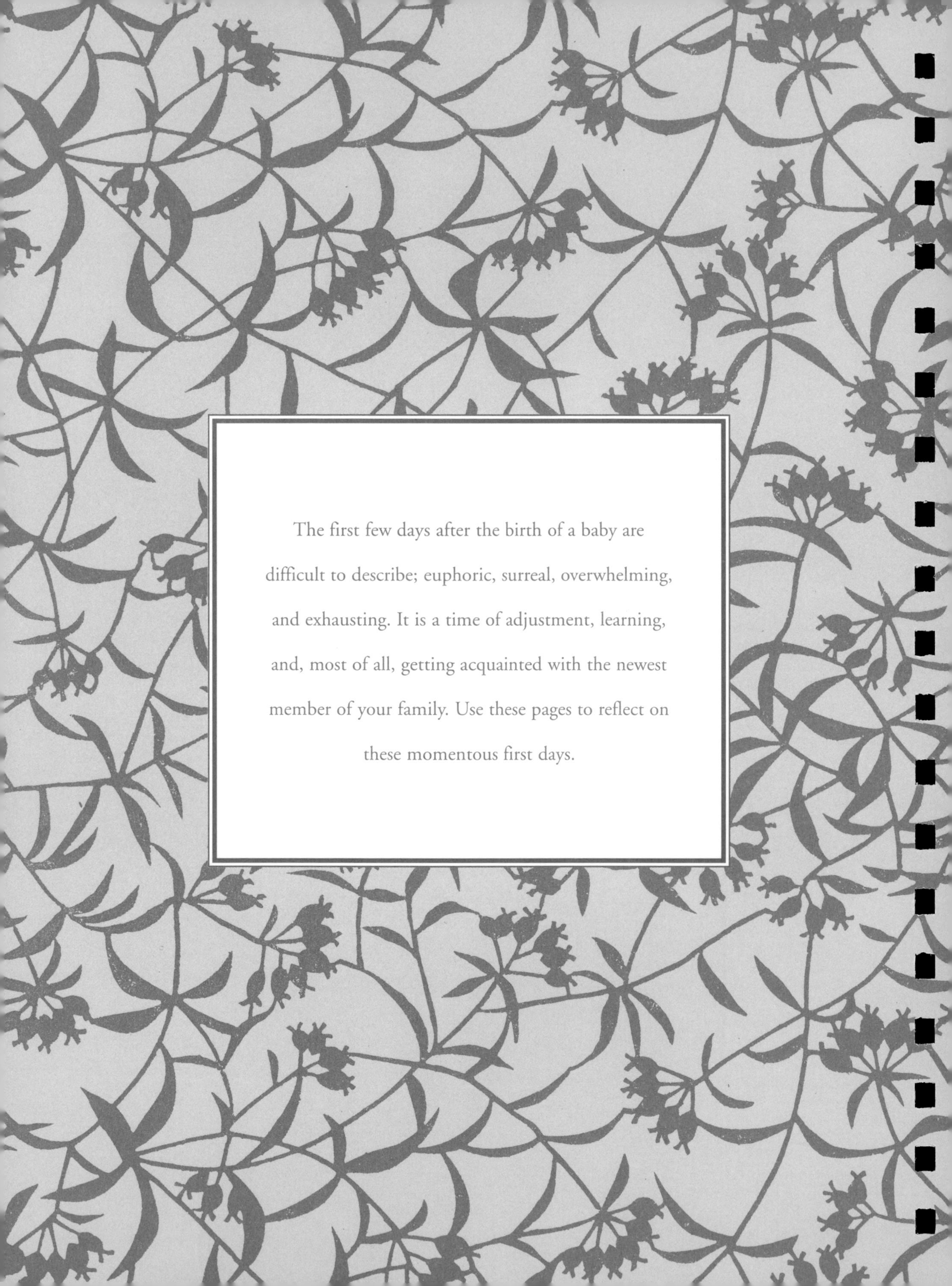

The first few days after the birth of a baby are difficult to describe; euphoric, surreal, overwhelming, and exhausting. It is a time of adjustment, learning, and, most of all, getting acquainted with the newest member of your family. Use these pages to reflect on these momentous first days.

going home

Date/Time

Baby's outfit

The car ride home

Address of baby's new home

How baby reacted to being home

Reactions from siblings or pets

Houseguests or helpers

Thoughts and feelings about bringing baby home

baby's first night home

Sleeping arrangements

Adjusting to a new family member

Memorable moments

baby's first days *settling in*

Feeding time

Changing time

Sleepy-time

Baby's disposition

Baby's visitors

postpartum

How my body is healing

How my body is feeling

Concerns about my health

Nursing notes

My overall emotional state

My worries

My joys

once in a lifetime

The time with your newborn will pass so quickly. There will be moments shared between you that you will hope never to forget. This is where you can reflect on all of the little things that you want to remember about this enchanting time in both your lives.

in conclusion

My thoughts and feelings about finishing this book

Last words

space for my family photograph

space for birth announcement or photographs